# AUTHENTICALLY YOU!

## AMELIA KRABACH

# INTRODUCTION

I started running in my mid-thirties, partly because I was a bit lost. It felt like I was searching for PURPOSE—some unattainable thing I couldn't quite grasp. Purpose was what I thought I was looking for, but as I began to find myself, I realized I was mistaken. I didn't know there were parts of me that were broken and others that hadn't been allowed to thrive. They were the reason I was chasing "purpose."

Through running seven marathons and twelve half-marathons, I discovered what I was truly made of, and the concept of *Authentically You!* took root. It won't take you running all those miles to reach that space, but it will take time.

This book is an adventure into the hidden crevices and cracks of yourself—parts of you yet to be explored. It's the unraveling of you. This journey can be both scary and exhilarating.

It reminds me of my favorite childhood book, *There's a Monster at the End of This Book*. In it, Grover spends the entire story worrying about the pages being turned and what might happen at the end. Each page turned is nerve-wracking and exciting, just like life.

Think of this book as a chance to discover yourself through a story. It's unconventional, but isn't life?

Wait a minute... my first character is already chiming in, eager to share her story. She's insisting I stop writing about myself and what you can gain from this book, and instead, let her take the stage. Her forceful nature is hard to ignore, and, well, that's part of the story. So, let's begin with her.

# CHAPTER 1

## MINDY (SHE/HER)

IT STARTED a few years ago when Mindy lost her parent. She didn't know exactly when it happened or how long she had been alone. What she did know was that it was time to find them.

Mindy is a brilliant child. She's a straight-A student who always finishes her homework on time. She spends her days reading, writing, and learning, and she loves taking on new tasks. She's also a master cleaner, dishwasher, and laundry folder.

But Mindy has another love: gossip. Not just the kind you hear from others, but the stories she tells herself, over and over. These stories are often about not being good enough or talking herself out of things—like finding her parent. The gossip can be overwhelming, filling hours of her day. She counters this by over-planning.

With so much time on her hands, Mindy became obsessed with planning everything—what to do, how to do it, and how to do it faster. It was this obsessive planning that eventually made her fixate on finding her parent.

She created spreadsheets and graphs detailing every date and time she remembered seeing her parent. She cleaned and organized every crevice of her home so that when she found them, they'd be proud of how tidy it was. Still, she felt stuck. So, she strategized, planned, and brainstormed even more ideas.

This planning consumed her entire weekend and bled into Monday morning. As the sun rose, she grabbed her books and spreadsheets, still thinking about her missing parent, and headed off to school.

# CHAPTER 2

## BRODY (THEY/THEM)

BRODY LIVED JUST across the street from Mindy. They didn't really talk to anyone, least of all Mindy. She was far too bossy for Brody's tastes. If you had to describe Brody in one word, it would be *basic*. They liked to keep life simple—eating, walking, and sleeping were their main priorities.

Brody never craved fancy foods, just the plain staples. They enjoyed taking walks, but not too far, and sleep was sacred. The key to keeping Brody happy was avoiding too much chaos or too many surprises.

Brody was also the kid who always seemed to need the bathroom at the worst possible moments. But once they'd gone, their mood usually improved—it helped them stay balanced.

Like Mindy, Brody had also lost their parent. The stress of it was wreaking havoc on them. Sometimes they couldn't sleep, and other times their body just didn't seem to cooperate. Brody thrived on consistency, and with their parent gone, everything felt out of sync.

This past weekend had only magnified the absence of their parent. Loud music from next door kept Brody up late on Saturday night. They'd run out of oatmeal, their breakfast staple, and the rainy weather meant they couldn't take their usual walks. These small disruptions stacked up until Brody reached a tipping point. It was clear, they needed to find their parent.

On Monday morning, Brody decided to take control. They dressed in comfortable clothes that felt good to move in, grabbed a banana as a substitute for oatmeal, and filled their water bottle. Carefully, they packed a healthy lunch and added extra water, just in case. With everything ready, Brody headed out the door, their mind set on what the day might bring.

# CHAPTER 3

## SAUL (HE/HIM)

SAUL LIVES next door to Brody and is the life of the party. Saul loves to stay up late, and this weekend was no different. He was jamming out and DJing his own house party. Saul is super creative and loves variety and fun.

Who wants to work hard when you can have fun? His motto is that he can always retake a class, but he can't relive a party. There is very little sleep in Saul's life, and his home is an absolute mess. He wishes he could travel and experience even more than what his life brings.

He used to be friends with Mindy from across the street when he was little and had his parent around, but his messiness these last few years annoyed Mindy, and she kept her distance. Brody, his other neighbor, really wasn't his friend. Not because they weren't nice—they were—it was because they were so boring. They really had nothing in common except being next-door neighbors.

This weekend, he realized that he really missed his parent. He, too, is parentless. He was all alone in his house without any friends, and it was really taking a toll on him. He knew if he had a parent around, they could drive him to all sorts of fun places, do fun things, and help him meet other cool kids like him.

Saul isn't a very good student, is always late, and sometimes even misses school altogether. Today was no different. He was busy trying to come up with an elaborate lunch with pickles, lunch meat, two different kinds of drinks, and candy—lots of candy. He didn't even notice the bus was already outside waiting for him, as usual.

He hurriedly put on various sorts of colorful clothing, grabbed his mishmash lunch, and headed out the door with his hair a total mess. He decided that today, of all days, was the perfect time to find his parent, especially since he was already on the bus without his homework.

# CHAPTER 4

THE BUS RIDE to school was chaotic as usual, with kids of various ages heading to Brown Elementary. Brody sat at the front of the bus, right behind the driver. Mindy carefully counted 13 rows and positioned herself by the window. Saul skipped to the very back of the bus to enjoy the rear view. With three stops left before arriving at school, each of them spent the time thinking about how to find their parent.

It was a memorable morning, not just because all three had decided to search for their parent, but also because spring was finally arriving in their town. The birds chirped louder than usual, and the kids on the bus mimicked their sounds with playful chatter. The noise was loud enough to distract even a diligent student like Mindy.

Already frustrated about her missing parent, Mindy found the noise around her unbearable. She pulled out her notebook and reviewed her list of possible places her parent could be. There were about twenty locations, but she felt it wasn't thorough enough and began adding more possibilities just in case.

The bus, warmed by the morning sun, made Brody uncomfortable enough to take off their jacket. Their anxiety about finding their parent only added to the discomfort. The tension had been interfering with their sleep and even their breathing. How could they possibly make it through the day? A sip of water seemed like a good idea to calm their nerves, but it only made them need the bathroom. Now, on top of their anxiety, they had a new problem. This day was shaping up to be a disaster.

Meanwhile, Saul daydreamed through the remaining bus stops, imagining his parent waiting at home for him after school, ready to plan all kinds of fun activities. Gazing out the back of the bus, he noticed the budding flowers and the sun warming the grass, with steam rising in the morning air. He thought about how to explain his forgotten homework to his teacher and decided that mentioning his missing parent might buy him some sympathy and time.

The bus came to a halt at school, and the kids filed off, ready to start their day. Saul, Mindy, and Brody grabbed their belongings and headed to class, each keeping their mission to find their parent a secret.

The first half of the day was unremarkable, a typical school morning that most kids would forget by the time they got home. That changed at lunchtime when news about three raccoons that had broken into the cafeteria over the weekend spread like wildfire. The gossip started quietly but quickly gained momentum after Mindy overheard two teachers talking about it. She made sure everyone in her class knew by passing notes and whispering the details.

The raccoons had managed to get into the freezers and pull out all the food, scattering it across the cafeteria floor. Maintenance hoped to trap the raccoons and clean up in time for lunch, but the mess proved too much. Animal control had been called, and lunch would have to be eaten in the classrooms.

Mindy was proud of being the first to spread the news but quickly realized the bad side of it—she had forgotten her lunch at home. What was she going to eat?

The classroom was beginning to stir from Mindy's gossip, and the teacher realized that the students were becoming aware of the situation involving the raccoons. Mindy, Saul, and Brody's teacher excused herself and headed out into the hallway.

The classroom got louder immediately as she left the room. Mindy started asking around to see who had brought a lunch and what was in that said lunch. She found out that Brody had a boring lunch but had brought plenty to share and had lots to drink, which made Mindy start to get thirsty. It was only water, but it would have to do. Brody was a little standoffish around her, but she would wear them down just enough to make them share their lunch with her.

She also found out that Saul had weird stuff and candy. Saul was a little out there, but Mindy knew that she could distract him and at least talk Saul into giving her some candy. As Mindy was finishing up her interrogation of kids in her classroom's lunches, their teacher came in and asked if everyone was willing to share their lunches as they were only able to get milk from the cafeteria before animal control got there.

Kids left and right started to share their sandwiches, and Brody reluctantly handed some of their food to Mindy and the extra bottle of water. Their teacher opened the windows to the outside, and groups of kids moved their desks closer to the windows to get some fresh air since recess and lunch was changed to classroom time.

Mindy, Saul, and Brody ended up sitting near each other, mostly because Mindy bossed them into it. She needed them for their lunch. It wasn't a shared experience, but this was an unexpected kind of day, so they accepted their fate.

Mindy proceeded to tell them all about herself during the lunch hour—how she had lost her parent and what plans she had for finding her parent. Saul was shocked. He, too, had a missing parent. Was Mindy more like him? Did they have something in common? Saul described his situation as well and mentioned that he was missing his parent too.

Brody was uncomfortable in this experience. They didn't really like to share anything about themselves, but they were also missing a parent. Should they tell them that? Quietly, Brody nodded their head in agreement, and Saul asked if they were in the same boat as well.

Brody softly spoke the word "yes," and a plan was hatched by Mindy to work together to each find their parent. Brody was still unsure about working with Mindy, but it was better than going about their day not doing anything.

After school, Saul said they would meet at his house to go over the plan. They each agreed right before an announcement was made that the raccoons were captured. It was turning out to be an eventful day.

# CHAPTER 5

AFTER SCHOOL, Mindy and Brody headed over to Saul's house to hatch a plan to find their parent. It was the least likely group to want to hang out together, but they all were desperate. Saul's house was a mess. There were clothes strewn all over the place in his bedroom. Cans of half-drunk Coke littered the tops of tables. The colored lights flickered and twinkled around the windows, making the room feel like it was a discotheque.

Brody was trying to find a chair with nothing on it. It was next to impossible to make space without moving at least five things out of the way. Mindy was feeling the need to clean. She was feeling a bit overwhelmed with the clutter and, at that moment, was at a loss for words.

This just made Saul grin. Both Brody and Mindy were out of their element, and this was just plain fun for Saul. He took his time gathering up some of his clothes and relished the quietness of Mindy.

Saul lost his interest in the search as soon as Brody asked to use the restroom. This was going to be work, Saul thought, and now

Mindy would have all of his attention since Brody just left the room.

Mindy directed her attention toward Saul and pulled out her list. "I have many places that we need to go to seek out my parent," Mindy said. "Maybe your parent will also be at those places as well." Her hands motioned emphatically as she spoke.

Saul was already getting distracted and tuning out Mindy's bossiness, but he figured trying out one of her ideas would get her off his back, so he agreed. When Brody got back from the bathroom, Saul and Mindy stood up and clued Brody in on the first location they would look for their parent.

They would look for their parent on Red Trail. The trail was right at the edge of town, where many people walked for adventure, solace, and exercise. Red Trail was a mountainous sort of trail and got treacherous, especially at night. It was imperative that they head over there soon since they only had a few hours before it got dark. Each of them headed back to their respective houses to gather what they thought they would need to help them on the trail.

Brody got back to their house needing a nap. Unfortunately, this was not going to be, as they knew Mindy would be pounding on their door in a matter of minutes. Brody put on some comfortable hiking shoes, grabbed extra water and a couple of bananas, placed them in their backpack, and headed out the door over to the sidewalk where they were to meet.

Mindy, on the other hand, grabbed maps, a compass, a flashlight, lighted headgear, a drone, hiking canes, and other various sorts of hiking gear. She zipped each item in individual bags, placed them all in her backpack—making sure the labels of each item were facing upright so that she could access them quickly—and headed out to the sidewalk. Brody walked out at the same time as Mindy, and they stood facing each other for a few minutes, waiting for Saul to come out of his home.

Standing outside waiting was painful for Mindy since she hated to be kept waiting. Brody took the time waiting to stretch their legs and eat a banana. Brody offered a banana to Mindy, but she was too preoccupied looking at her maps to want to eat.

Eventually, Saul came out of his house with nothing but binoculars. "Don't you want something to drink for later?" Brody asked Saul. Saul gave Brody a surprised look and went back into the house to grab a Coke. Mindy also went back into her house and grabbed something to drink as well.

When they all had enough hydration for their hike to find their parent, they set off toward Red Trail.

# CHAPTER 6

SAUL WAS ACTUALLY EXCITED to head to Red Trail. It was a really cool place with lots of sections of trail that split off into other trails. Some of it went along the river, while other parts of it went up a cliffy area with large rocks. Saul couldn't wait to use his binoculars to check out the various wildlife that was there. He had heard in school that there were some new baby eagles that were born in January and that they might be spotted learning to fly soon.

There was some disagreement over what area they should hike through first, but they ended up deferring to Mindy since it was her idea to visit the trail. Brody was already cautious and asking how far they think they might walk. Mindy was in no mood to listen to Brody this early in the hike because they hadn't even walked 100 feet. She walked ahead so that she wouldn't have to answer Brody and to lead the group.

This made Brody sulk a bit, but they continued on just the same. The trees in the woods were gaining leaves by the day as the spring weather was helping make the forest a forest again. The denseness of the leaves made it feel a bit scarier since you couldn't make out where the path led. Saul was skipping along the trail right behind Mindy, and Brody was following in the rear.

Mindy was face-first in the maps, trying to identify what trail she was on and which trail would be the one she would hike next. Saul was too busy looking around and enjoying the wildlife that he was open to just observing and having fun. Brody was hydrating so that they could keep up with whatever was in store for them. It was three kids, all with separate agendas, walking on a singular path leading to who knows where.

Mindy was starting to get a little testy. She had already dragged the group down a few paths, and the next one seemed harder with a much bigger incline. Saul was not having any fun at this point. He had already walked farther than he wanted to and still had no sight of the eagle's nest or his parent. Brody was tired. They really needed that nap after school today, and now, a few hours later, walking around in circles was not helping their mood.

Each of them was tiring of each other, and it was starting to get dark. Mindy pulled out her flashlight and looked over the map, realizing she missed a turn and was completely lost. This put Brody into a panic, and they started to cry. Saul was frustrated, so he sat down in the middle of the pathway and started to draw in the dirt with a stick.

It was a complete nightmare. They had no luck, not even a clue, in finding their parent, and now they were lost in the middle of the woods, and neither of them had a solution.

The three of them wandered around aimlessly until they came upon a bench with a runner tying her shoe. She looked like she knew where she was going, but none of them wanted to ask for help.

The runner looked up at them, acknowledged them, and went back to tying her shoe. It was a pivotal moment where any one of them should have asked for help, but each kid was stuck in their own trauma and didn't even think to ask.

The runner got up from the seat and headed left down a trail. Saul saw her bright pink shoes and immediately was distracted enough to go off from the group and follow her. Brody and Mindy snapped out of their tantrums and followed Saul closely behind.

Saul continued to follow the runner, with Mindy and Brody closely behind, all the way out of the Red Trail back to the entrance. They weren't lost anymore, and each of them breathed a sigh of relief. Thanks to that female runner in the bright pink shoes, they were able to get back to the entrance. Each of them was internally thankful that she happened to be at the end of her run, not the beginning.

They all decided that the search for their parent today should end since they were luckily not lost anymore. Before heading back to their respective houses, they each agreed that tomorrow after school they would meet on the sidewalk to continue the search for their parent.

# CHAPTER 7

SAUL ENDED up skipping school that day. The day was up in the air as to whether everyone would be looking for their parent. Mindy and Brody acknowledged each other on the bus ride to school and got through the day on their own.

After school, Brody was pretty tired and, once again, needed a nap. Brody had only been in their house for fifteen minutes when Mindy knocked on the door. Brody reluctantly opened it and joined Mindy out on the sidewalk to look for their parent again. Mindy was trying to decide whether she should bother Saul since he never made it to school. Brody was pretty checked out and didn't care one way or another.

Mindy knocked on Saul's door repeatedly for what seemed like five minutes. A frustrated Saul opened the door. He was still in his pajamas and looked like he hadn't slept. He had dried paint on his fingers and was listening to loud music.

"Are you coming or what?" Mindy asked Saul.

Saul took a moment to process what Mindy was saying, then

hurriedly closed the door. Brody was confused, and Mindy just shrugged her shoulders and stepped off the front porch.

"I guess he's not coming," Mindy said to Brody as she continued walking down the street.

As Brody was contemplating staying home as well—since they were so tired from the previous day's hike—Saul came running out the door. Still in his pajamas, Saul caught up to the two of them, and they continued down the street.

"I thought you weren't coming," Mindy said to Saul.

Saul ignored Mindy and walked over to Brody.

"This is no fun," Saul said to Brody, who agreed that looking for their parent was exhausting. The two of them reluctantly followed Mindy down the street without asking where she was heading.

Brody finally spoke up and told Mindy that they were tired and only wanted to look for an hour. Mindy half-heartedly nodded in agreement, but Brody wasn't so sure she was totally on board with their decision.

Up ahead was a park that Mindy wanted to check out to see if her parent was there. The park had swings, tennis courts, and a running track. There were many people around, and Mindy set off looking.

As Brody and Saul stood in the field, Saul noticed that the swings were empty and that the same runner girl with the bright pink shoes from yesterday was over by the swings, drinking from her water bottle.

This is weird, Saul thought as he headed over to the swings.

Brody, still exhausted from the previous day and now thirsty as well, followed him. Still in his pajamas, Saul grabbed the middle swing and started swinging back and forth, kicking his feet higher and higher. The runner girl stared at him in amusement and continued drinking her water.

Brody leaned against the post of the swing set and tried not to stare at the girl drinking water. The runner girl looked at them and noticed that Brody was staring at her.

She immediately mentioned that she had an extra bottle of water if they were thirsty. Brody didn't know what to do. Should they tell her that they were dying of thirst or not? She was a stranger, but Brody was so thirsty.

The runner girl pulled out an extra, unopened bottle of water without saying anything and handed it to Brody. Brody was amazed and graciously accepted the drink. He immediately downed it and felt a bit more energized.

The runner girl finished her drink, closed the cap on the bottle, and headed off into the distance.

Brody took the swing next to Saul and just sat. It was nice to take a break and wait for Mindy while she looked for her parent. Mindy was walking around frantically, looking at each and every person to see if they might be her parent. She also walked the entire perimeter for clues. Watching her was exhausting for both Saul and Brody.

Both tried to prod each other to leave the swing set and get Mindy to head home, but the comfort of the swings kept them there.

It had now been two hours since they had left their homes, and still, there was no sign of anyone's parent.

Mindy finally came over to the swing set with a disgusted look. She was angry and mad that the others hadn't helped. That seemed to be their cue to get up from the swings and head back home with her.

The entire walk home was unpleasant, as Mindy did all the yelling while the other two just tried not to get in her way.

Each of them went home and closed their doors without saying goodbye.

# CHAPTER 8

A FEW DAYS passed before Brody approached Mindy at school. No one had spoken since Tuesday, and now it was already Friday. Brody was having a hard time without a parent. Mindy looked up and accepted Brody's extra banana. She peeled it back and took a big bite just as Saul walked up behind her. It was a comical scene because Mindy had taken too big of a bite and couldn't talk, which made them all start laughing.

That eased the tension between the three. Brody offered Saul a piece of fruit as well, knowing he would find bananas boring, so they grabbed a kiwi from home instead. Saul was intrigued and commented to Brody that a kiwi tasted like a mix of banana and strawberry. It was an interesting flavor that Saul quite enjoyed.

Brody already felt better knowing the three of them weren't fighting anymore. The idea of bringing fruit to school for each other was perfect—it served as an icebreaker. Now, they could get back to searching for their parent.

Saul agreed that they should meet again after school and try an indoor location this time. He thought that maybe one of their parents would be somewhere indoors, and the YMCA in Midtown seemed like a good place to check.

After school, the three of them walked a few blocks west to the YMCA. Inside, a large hallway directed them to the main area where the basketball courts were located. Down the left hallway were various after-school classrooms and the stairs leading to the pool. To the right, another hallway led to the main workout area, where rows of treadmills and rowing machines lined up behind a half-wall.

The group decided to start looking in the workout area. Saul spotted the running lady from the other day on a treadmill and decided to be a bit silly, pretending to walk down imaginary stairs in front of her. Mindy, always up for being silly, joined him. Brody, however, just stood there, amazed at the runner's stamina.

The running lady chuckled at the two of them messing around and slowed down her pace on the treadmill. It was just enough of a pause for her to recognize them.

The treadmill came to a complete stop, and she stepped off, wiping her face with a towel. Brody wondered if she was done with her workout or if they had interrupted her. She didn't seem annoyed, so it must have been perfect timing.

The woman walked over to the group and asked if they needed something. Mindy was completely tongue-tied by the woman's sudden attention, so Brody decided to speak for the group.

"Hi, I'm Brody, and this is Mindy and Saul. We've been on a quest to find our parent, and since we keep running into you, we thought maybe you could help."

The woman took a moment to absorb what was said, then reluctantly agreed to meet them the following morning at Red Trail to assist in their search. She introduced herself as Amelia and told them to meet her at the trail entrance at 8 a.m. on Saturday.

The group was excited. They now had an adult willing to help—maybe not an overly enthusiastic one, but still an adult. It felt like progress. Tomorrow seemed more promising by the minute, so they stopped their search for the day and headed back home.

# CHAPTER 9

SATURDAY MORNING CAME EARLY for Saul. He made it a point to set two alarms to help wake himself up. The 8 a.m. time wasn't impossible for Saul, but he liked to take his time getting up and ready in the mornings. Amelia had mentioned wearing tennis shoes and clothes suitable for outdoor running, so Saul wandered around the house, trying to put together some kind of outfit.

Brody, on the other hand, had already had coffee, toast with peanut butter, and put on their outfit for the day by 7:30 a.m. They had gotten enough sleep since they hadn't been out too late searching for their parent the night before. Mindy was ready as well, and the three of them met outside before heading to the base of Red Trail.

Amelia was already there waiting for them. She let them know that if they ran, they could cover more ground and explore more of the trails. Eager to impress her, the kids agreed.

The four of them took off into the woods at a fairly fast pace. Mindy immediately started asking all kinds of questions—what

Amelia was thinking, which trails they were taking, and how far they were going to run. It was super distracting for Saul and Brody, causing them to slow down as a result of Mindy's excessive talking.

At first, Amelia was patient with Mindy, but as the questions kept coming, she started to get annoyed. She noticed that the other two kids were slowing down, and she began to suspect that Mindy's constant chatter was affecting their pace.

Around mile three, Amelia slowed down to match Saul and Brody's speed and asked how they were doing. The boys were astonished that the "runner lady" even cared, and it actually motivated them to try keeping up with her pace again.

As they ran, Saul pointed out various types of wildlife and trees that interested him. The group took in the beauty of the trail on that peaceful Saturday morning. For a brief moment, there was an ease among them—it felt like they could really work together and maybe, just maybe, find their parent.

Unfortunately, Brody threw a wrench into their run. They needed a bathroom—and not just a quick stop. Brody needed to go number two, and an actual restroom had to be found immediately.

Amelia, worried, started searching for one of those less-than-ideal portable toilets while Brody looked more and more desperate. It was stressful for the whole group to stop what they were doing to hunt for a bathroom, and they almost didn't find one in time.

Despite the minor crisis, they considered it a small triumph to have made it through their first experience together without an accident—though they still had no luck in finding their parent.

Amelia decided they should meet back at the trail the next day but at a later time. Since it would be Sunday, she figured there might be more people around.

# CHAPTER 10

SAME TRAIL AND SAME GROUP. The following day, they all met wearing similar outfits from yesterday. The only difference was their attitudes—no one seemed to want to be there, including Amelia.

It was an absolutely gorgeous day, and many people were walking about with families and pets, enjoying the trails. The four of them laced up their shoes and started out in a jog, with Amelia leading.

Saul was internally struggling with the same trail again. It was too boring for his liking, and he was getting frustrated with no sign of finding his parent. He couldn't see past his shoes to look around and enjoy the day. He was really depressed and agitated.

Brody was actually a bit sore from the day before but overall in good spirits, since they knew what the terrain was like and what to expect. This calmed their nerves down a bit, and they were open to another jog with Amelia.

Mindy was already wondering aloud why they were running in the same direction and if they could actually run farther today.

Mindy really wanted to go farther than the day before and would not stop going on and on about it.

Amelia was starting to question why she even went out today with this motley crew. It was like herding cats with the three of them, and it was becoming exhausting. She tried ignoring them, but each one acted out even more—Mindy asked more questions, Saul complained, and Brody just tried to keep up, stopping a few times to stretch their legs.

The run and search were not making sense for any of them, so Amelia stopped running and just continued to walk instead. That seemed to work, and each of them started to look around. Up ahead, there was a cave that none of them had ever seen before, and it seemed like a perfect place to go exploring.

Amelia headed that way, and the rest of them followed. They were much more enthusiastic about the cave than about running, and Amelia seemed satisfied. The cave had various mosses growing around it and light purple flowers in the cracks of the rock. It was seemingly magical, and the group continued to explore more, following the trail of the cave out through the other side.

On the other side was the cliff, which led down to the path that they had run on the other day. It was a perfect time to take in the sights and look around at the various people in the distance. This day was starting to get a little better from exploring, and Amelia made the decision to head back, taking a slow jog before everyone's moods changed again.

# CHAPTER 11

THE FOLLOWING DAY, Amelia made an executive decision not to run. Sunday's run had not been very productive, and the group was a little too hostile to run another one so soon. She decided to spend some time with Mindy, Saul, and Brody to get to know them better. She met them at the school track field that day and planned to show them some yoga moves she had recently learned.

Amelia put on some music from her phone. At first, it was relaxing spa music, but everyone internally wanted something different. Amelia noticed this without anyone saying anything and changed it to salsa music. The group instantly started laughing and became more open to learning the Downward Dog and Cat-Cow poses.

It got quite loud with Mindy barking, Brody meowing, and Saul mooing. The music in the background made the experience even weirder. Amelia was glad they were alone, yet not alone at the same time. It was freeing and fun to be silly while stretching their bodies.

Everyone started talking loudly and expressing themselves to Amelia, and she actually felt a turning point in the case to find their parent. Each of them was becoming more open with her, and Amelia knew that if they trusted her more, she could help them find what they were looking for.

Amelia needed to think of a way to get them to trust her and open up about what they needed and who they really were. She remembered her past love of being on stage—the thrill and fear of the unknown audience. Maybe if she found a way to get each of them on stage, they would reveal more about who they were and what they were like.

Yoga had proven to be a good choice in getting the group to open up. Now, Amelia just needed to get the crew to meet up after school to introduce them to some "theater." She made a promise to herself to get them to the auditorium soon.

Before they left the field, Saul approached Amelia privately. He mentioned that he hadn't stopped thinking about the cave and somehow believed that was where he had last seen his parent. Amelia agreed to take them back tomorrow after school to revisit the cave.

# CHAPTER 12

BACK TO THE woods they went. It was Saul who was feeling the attachment to where the cave was. He needed to get back there and see if that was where he remembered seeing his parent last. He was so drawn to the energy there, and exploring the cave the other day stirred something inside of him. Was he getting close to finding his parent?

Mindy had already calculated where the cave was last seen, so they had to run about 2.5 miles. Brody had a sore knee, so the group had to run a little slower. Amelia was helping to wrap Brody's knee to help it absorb some of the pain and make them run better. Brody thought it was a loving gesture, but they really just wanted to rest.

Saul wanted to get to the spot as soon as possible since it was all he could think about at school. He daydreamed the day away, thinking of all the different kinds and colors of moss with the pretty flowers. Maybe if he had just been in nature all day instead of school, he would be much happier, and being happy would draw his parent out to find him.

They hadn't even started the run to the cave, and already, it felt like a huge job. Everybody wished they had a time machine to get to the cave without the work. The almost three miles to the cave were wearing on each of them, including Saul, who had wanted to go there in the first place.

Saul figured that this might be his last opportunity to check out the cave before everyone protested to never going back to that space again. He had to make it there and enjoy most of it as long as he could. He would wait to drag out the day when he got there. It was better not to get the group knowing ahead of time his plans or else they may not even go at all. He knew it was sort of deceitful but he wanted to get his way this time, especially since he was starting to get his feelings back.

They ran for the most part to the cave and stopped a few times for Brody to catch their breath and rub their knee a little. The cave wasn't as glamorous as the first time they saw it but it was still worth seeing and viewing.

Saul stopped and began moving his hands along the moss and noticed the softness of it. It was comforting and he remembered doing things with his parent in nature. He loved the contrast of colors and he was remembering his parent did as well. It was so long ago when his parent just took the time to feel and enjoy the nature. He could hardly remember it but still it resonated with him in his core. He sat down near the entrance and listened to the chirping of the birds.

Mindy already was going over the almost three mile run with the group on how they could run better and faster. She was chattering on about not beating their last time and that they would need to run this faster next time in order to add more miles. It really put a damper in everyone's mood.

Brody was just thankful to be resting. The knee was not feeling any better and running almost three miles back was going to not be pleasant. Brody propped up their feet along the cave and the knee was starting to feel better. The elevation was helping drain the swelling out of it. Brody was perfectly content in that position while the rest of the group worked on clues.

Saul only had Mindy to convince to hang around longer and the best way to keep her in one position was to ask her questions. He remembered from their friendship long ago that if he kept asking her questions, she would go on tangents to try to figure out the answer. That was good for at least an hour longer in the cave.

The first question he asked Mindy was whether she thought this cave was a portal to another universe. He couldn't help but laugh as he asked it knowing full well that he wouldn't have to ask another question until they needed to leave. Mindy went on a tangent discussing and analyzing the question and replaying in her mind other times she thought about this same topic. An hour went by, and Saul's feeling of home started to magnify. He knew this cave was part of a clue. He just needed to find more clues until he found his parent.

Amelia was a little distant over the past hour in the cave. She wasn't able to communicate to them what was going on in her head and she hurriedly made everyone get up and head back. Brody was really stiff and took their time getting up, in which Amelia snapped a bit at them. It was a little unsettling, but they pushed themselves to get up and try to block the pain. Mindy was still talking about the universe and now worrying about time travel back to the entrance.

Saul took in the memory of this experience and slowly joined the group. The run back was quiet as each of them bottled up their feelings about the day.

# CHAPTER 13

BRODY COULDN'T UNDERSTAND why they had been crying the following day. Amelia talked about maybe taking the day to herself because she was due for her monthly cycle and needed to be alone with her thoughts. Was Brody going to have this experience as well? Brody had no clue what cycle she was talking about, but it made them emotional every time they thought about Amelia not feeling well.

Since Amelia wanted to be alone, Brody had invited Mindy and Saul to their house after school. The only problem was that Brody wasn't sure what to make of all this crying. It was quite embarrassing to have all of the waterworks and no idea where it was coming from. Maybe Mindy would know what to do, or at least have read about this condition, Brody thought.

Mindy and Saul joined Brody at their house. It was an economical home with minimal furnishings. The couch was at least comfortable to Saul's tastes, and the TV was a decent size with some basic channel programming.

As Brody discussed their emotions with the two of them, Mindy remembered for a moment that her parent also experienced that cycle thing, and maybe that was the reason she left. It made Mindy start worrying about what they should or shouldn't ask Amelia when they saw her next.

Mindy's worrying made her anxious. She was now going over every conversation she had with Amelia and what might have led her to need to be alone. It was very unsettling for everyone in the room, partly because neither Saul nor Brody knew what to do to get Mindy to calm down.

Saul just wanted to sit and watch TV and veg. He really couldn't deal with his emotions and doing nothing was better than feeling anything. He was already overwhelmed with Mindy worrying and Brody crying. Avoidance was the next best thing. He surfed through the limited channel selection on Brody's television and settled on Road Trip Antiquing.

The show had various people traveling all over the world buying things and reselling them. It seemed interesting enough since each show was different, and that appealed to Saul. Brody just enjoyed not being alone and being able to rest on the couch, and Mindy got distracted enough with learning that she stopped worrying for the time being.

Each of them sat in silence, absorbing the TV show, feeling a little better being with others, even if some of them were still alone in their own thoughts. They sat there for hours, and eventually their emotions or lack of emotions settled.

# CHAPTER 14

A FEW DAYS LATER, Amelia showed up outside Mindy, Brody, and Saul's school to see if they wanted to run into town and see the sights. Amelia was missing her newfound friends, and the three of them hadn't done anything productive in finding their parent since Amelia went M.I.A.

Each of them had luckily been wearing clothes to run in since the school had game days with events of all sorts at school. What perfect synchronism, and they dropped their book bags off in her car and went for a run.

Mindy wanted to ask about the week and why Amelia had stopped communicating but thought better of it since she was in a good mood. Instead, Mindy took on the job of planning the run and where they would be heading. Mindy loved to figure out the distance, time, and places to run. She was in her element. Today, the rest of the gang went along with it with no complaints.

Brody was feeling much better since they had cried it out the past few days. The knee was also stronger and less achy since they took a few days off from exercise. Overall, Brody was feeling more balanced than they had been in a while.

Saul was just excited to be able to not have to deal with Mindy and Brody's emotions. The last few days were a bit awkward for Saul, and the only saving grace was that one tv show they agreed on watching together. He was glad to have Amelia back and was looking forward to doing something different today, even if they were running. Saul didn't hate running; he just thought it was boring. It was, however, the perfect experience to see more interesting things, which Saul loved.

The run happened to be on a busy street. It was a gorgeous day, and many cars had their windows down with their music blaring. Some cars had cute dogs with their faces hanging out, other cars had their convertible tops down. It was a perfect day for Saul to spend the day away looking about. This made him really happy and then he started to get emotional.

Why was he all of a sudden getting emotional? That was the one thing he took pride in: avoidance. Now, he couldn't shut it off. He was connecting to the storylines of various people in their cars and what they might be feeling. He tried to look away and focus on the group and run, but he couldn't. Even Amelia joined him in the observing, and she too was feeling it.

Mindy, however, was letting everyone know that they needed to step up their pace to get to the destination. Saul had no idea what destination she was talking about but it seemed important to her. He tried to listen and start running faster, but the dog in the one car kept distracting him. It wasn't until the dog was out of sight that Saul finally joined in with the pace set by Mindy.

Brody was just content with being in the group. They were surprised at the halfway point when Amelia pulled out a snack and drink for everyone. Brody was just thinking about how thirsty and hungry they were getting and voila, Amelia had replenishments.

Amelia paused the time on her running watch which helped Mindy with her anxiousness of getting a good time and they all had a snack and drink together. Amelia took this moment to tell them that she had a surprise for them and that she would meet them after class tomorrow to show them the surprise.

Brody hated surprises. They wanted to know what was happening to them at all times. Brody wished that Amelia just told them now what it was instead of waiting for tomorrow. Brody wasn't feeling the run now and wanted to go home.

Saul and Mindy got excited about the surprise. Mindy started coming up with all sorts of ideas of what it might be and Saul just wished Mindy wouldn't figure it out before the actual surprise happened.

The run back was harder than Amelia thought. Maybe she shouldn't have told them about the surprise so soon since now that is all they could think about and the run was turning into a jog/walk. Mindy was disappointed that their time was not good and Brody was uneasy about the surprise and Saul was.. who knows where Saul was…

The group realized that Saul was not there at the end. Where had they lost him? Amelia turned around and started walking back to where she last saw him and came up to him leaning on a tree. He was batting with a stick the leaves of the tree. It was so random and Amelia was puzzled on how he got so distracted.

Amelia asked Saul what was the matter and Saul said he had no idea. He was feeling everything around him and when that happened he just wanted to stop and do nothing. Amelia coaxed him out from under the tree and slowly walked him back to the car where the others were waiting. Amelia assured Saul that tomorrow's surprise would help him with the feelings he was starting to notice.

Everyone headed home and agreed to meet, even the reluctant ones, after school tomorrow.

# CHAPTER 15

BRODY, Saul and Mindy couldn't wait until after school for their surprise from Amelia. Two of them were excited and one just wanted to get it over with. Amelia told them that she wanted them to trust her and this surprise would help in that endeavor.

After school, Amelia was waiting outside and ushered them right back into their school. Saul was already a little bit skeptical. What kind of surprise is at school? He couldn't think of one thing that was fun or surprising in school.

Brody and Mindy didn't complain but also with their guards up walked behind Amelia back into the school and into the auditorium. The auditorium was empty with the main lights focused on the stage with the red curtains closed.

Amelia asked the three of them to walk up the stairs on to the stage and behind the red curtain. She asked each one of them to take a moment and do anything they wanted on stage to show her who they really were. Amelia said that she would be there in the audience to support them in their moment on stage and that they could really trust her.

Of course, Mindy instantly took the center of stage and the other two reluctantly went to the sides of the theater. The curtain opened and out there all by herself was Mindy with the spotlight directly shining on her. Mindy always had a plan. She was usually ready and this time she froze. She stood out there with nothing. She stared directly out into the audience and could barely see the outline of Amelia. It was scary and she started to panic.

But then all of sudden she heard clapping. It was Amelia clapping for her. This helped her and she started to name out loud all the presidents in order. She started putting down outlines for books she wanted to write on big white boards. Mindy was on fire. She was now attempting to fill the whole stage with things she learned and what she wanted to accomplish. It was calming her, and she had tremendous focus while she heard Amelia's clapping. The curtain began to close on Mindy, and she was a bit dejected because her time was up, but she was also feeling really happy for the first time in a long time.

Out in the audience Saul's name was mentioned and in response he slowly sauntered out onto the stage as the curtains were opening for his moment. Saul started singing various songs making up the verses since he couldn't remember the actual words. He was being silly, and he noticed Amelia laughing out in the audience. This got Saul to start doing cartwheels and acting out parts to Broadway shows. He started to move props out onto the stage to use in his acting debut and was enjoying the smiles and out loud laughter coming from the audience of one. It was inspiring him to create and make a magical experience on the stage. He was caught up in the experience so much that he didn't even notice that the red curtains were closing and his time was up.

Mindy seemed a bit irritated since now there was odd trinkets and props left out on stage for Brody and that didn't seem fair. She started to quickly shove some of it off of stage and Saul reluctantly joined in helping her.

The curtain remained closed for a bit until Brody heard their name. It was perfect timing since the stage was now cleared for Brody's moment. As the curtain opened Brody started to breathe deeply focusing on their breath and taking in the moment. Amelia stood up and gave Brody a standing ovation. They were astonished.

How could they deserve that kind of praise for just deep breathing? It made Brody take notice what else their body could do. Brody started to stretch and lunge imitating Mindy's arm movements from earlier and Saul's dance moves from a moment ago. Amelia's applause helped to make it such a calming experience. The fear of the surprise went away and they enjoyed their time on stage. The red curtain closed again as they stood there wondering what was going to happen next.

Amelia joined them behind the red curtain and asked each one of them to form a circle around her holding hands. Mindy's hand was forcefully locked on Brody's and Saul loosely joined the two. After a few minutes of being forced to hold hands, each one of them started to relax and the holding of hands began to feel more comfortable.

Neither person had a firmer grip than another. They were all holding hands equally. Amelia slowly turned in the middle of the circle looking into each one of their eyes to let them know that they could trust her. It was time to work together. Each of them were as important as the other and they needed to treat each other in the same manner.

It was a really special moment. They were being treated as important individuals working as a team. Amelia and the gang exited out of the auditorium inspired for the first time in a long time.

Amelia was right, Brody thought, this was a really good surprise.

# CHAPTER 16

THE NEXT MORNING, Amelia swung by and picked up Brody, Mindy and Saul to take them to school. The kids were excited that someone other than themselves had taken an interest in them. It was a perfect morning as they stopped for breakfast on the way to school. Amelia treated them to a balanced meal.

The group seemed to be getting along. Yes, they had their differences but not one person in particular needed to take over and let their needs be more important than another. Amelia went over the day's events and got everyone to agree to going for a run near the river to venture out in their search.

This would happen earlier today since they had a half day of school. Amelia realized that she needed them more than she thought in helping her in her runs. This was a win/win situation. They would be her running companion while she helped find what they were looking for.

Just around the noon hour, Amelia picked them up and headed down towards the river for an afternoon five mile run. When they got to the parking lot of the riverfront walk, Brody was already asking when they could get lunch.

Interestingly enough, Amelia thought about getting breakfast for the group but completely forgot about lunch. This was going to put a damper in getting the run in before it got too hot. She remembered that she had a protein bar in her glove compartment and went back to the car to retrieve it.

She handed it over to Brody and they took a bite. Brody offered it as well to Mindy and Saul and they took a bite as well finishing off the protein bar. Amelia vowed to get a big lunch after they went out for their run.

The group headed out along the river bank towards the willow trees as Saul got Amelia to play a musical playlist that motivated everyone. Mindy was asked to keep track of the distance and to let Amelia know when they got to 2.5 miles so that they could turn back around and head back to the car.

This day was working out so smoothly. The kids were starting to trust Amelia and she was relying on their input more. Amelia took the five mile run in stride and checked in with each of them at various points of the run.

Brody sometimes wanted to slow down. Mindy needed reassurance that she was following directions well. Saul was encouraged to sing along with the playlist whenever he felt like it. Each of them were being heard on this run and Amelia was feeling like this was her best run ever.

When they got back from the run, no one noticed that they hadn't spent time looking for their parent. They were caught up with the experience at hand and Amelia had made them feel special.

It wasn't until the next day that Mindy, Saul and Brody remembered that they didn't look for their parent. Now they were in a sabotaging mode. Why should they go for any more runs with Amelia if she isn't going to help them? This made Mindy angry.

Mindy just wanted to go on thinking a repetitive thought and ignore any learning at school. She couldn't get out of her own way. She just kept thinking on repeat. Her thoughts really didn't make sense. It was as if she was a broken record. Over and over again she thought about the whys. Why is Amelia in her life? Why hasn't she found her parent? Why won't Amelia help her? Why? Why? Why?

Saul wasn't any better at school that day. He was daydreaming the day away. He just wanted to be anywhere other than at school. He was feeling an emotional loss at something. He had no idea what that was but it was missing and he was feeling it. He was so sad at being stuck in school with this emotion and had no idea what to do about it.

Brody, too, was feeling something. They were extremely exhausted. tired from everything and nothing. Brody was comfortable with Amelia and when they were around her, felt reassured. Somehow, they still had this exhaustion coming over them and it was probably more about the lost parent than anything else. How could Brody get Amelia to care just as much about their lost parent as she did with them?

When Amelia saw them again after school, everyone was quiet. Not one of them mentioned what was going on with them and Amelia could sense something was not quite right. She didn't question them or pry. She just let them be and dropped them off at their homes.

This sabotaging episode went on for an additional day. Brody, Saul and Mindy got up the next day and continued with their drama filled school day the same as before. It wasn't until day three that Amelia on the way to school with Mindy, Brody and Saul stopped the car and questioned them.

Amelia realized they were all sabotaging their happiness and connection. Day three was the final straw. She needed to confront the kids and find out how to help. She turned towards the three of them in the back seat of the car and asked why they were sabotaging themselves?

Neither of them spoke up. They were traumatized and afraid to speak. It would mean that they had to tell Amelia that she wasn't listening and they didn't want to disappoint her. Luckily, Amelia realized that she needed to make the first move.

She asked them to forgive her. She apologized for not listening to them in the past but that she was going to make an effort. Amelia asked that they come out into the open and speak freely. She knew she had to comfort them and love on them for a few minutes and she did just that.

She had them get out of the car and gave each of them a hug and held them for a few minutes.

She told them that she wasn't perfect or healed but she was working on herself and that she needed them in her life.

Did they want to be part of that? Some parts of them weren't on board. She asked them to let those parts go. Maybe those parts aren't helping them. Mindy took out one of her diaries and placed it on the picnic table. She said she kept reading that diary over and over and it wasn't a good time in her life and she didn't need to remember it anymore. Amelia took that as a good sign and motioned for her to discard it into the garbage can nearby.

Brody took a moment and watched Mindy. They followed quickly after and barfed into the garbage can. They were feeling so much emotion it was making them sick. The moment Brody barfed, they started to feel so much better. The exhaustion lifted and they were feeling more calm. It was a release of the last few days of turmoil.

Amelia had Saul imagine the parts of him that were emotionally stuck looking for the lost parent riding away on a dragon out into the distance. The emotional feeling of loss wasn't helping Saul find his parent or get along with the others so it needed to fly away on a dragon. He noticed that he got more present in the moment the minute the dragon flew away with his old emotions.

All three of them were more settled after Amelia took the time to have them forgive her and help them release some of the past muddled parts. They each openly got back into the car and headed to school with renewed interest and a more trusting sense of belonging.

As she dropped them off, Amelia promised that she would make a more concerted effort to help them on their quest.

# CHAPTER 17

THE WEEKEND WAS upon them and a new day with a new view of each other was taking place. It meant a lot to them to have Amelia take the time out and let them know that she was willing to finally listen and hear what they had to contribute.

This was a new experience for all of them and it was going to take a day at a time for them to slowly move into a trusting relationship.

Mindy was so different from Brody who was complete opposite of Saul. The trio of mismatched kids seemed to be getting along because of Amelia. She was the glue that held them together, a leader of sorts.

Yes, they all had the same problem, the problem of the missing parent. Amelia wondered how she could really get them to work together? The possibility of spending at least 10-15 minutes a day fulfilling one of their needs individually would help them feel like they were being heard and that would get them to work together, she thought.

What were their differences? Amelia took a moment to process their differences.

Mindy was a strong-willed person. She seemed to prosper when she was learning something or doing something with her mind. Her only downfall was her repetitive thinking. The constant gossip that Mindy gravitated towards generally got her in trouble and it made the others not like her that much.

Brody needed sleep, much more than the other two. In fact, the other two probably didn't sleep much. Brody also needed to eat at a more scheduled time and it needed to be more nourishing. The healthier the better and basic was actually recommended. Brody was the balanced one and probably the one no one listened to when it came to making a decision. Brody also needed to move. They really didn't like being lazy but didn't want to overdo it. This was a good thing, Amelia thought. She would try to listen more to Brody in the future, for balance.

Saul was the wild card. Saul didn't know one minute from one hour. He was really good at getting Amelia to spend more time just enjoying life although she needed to be more time oriented around him in the future because he could be super distracting.

So today, Amelia gave Mindy a task to come up with places that the group would be searching for their parent today, keeping in mind the differences in each person. Mindy went right to work at the picnic table and started listing places where Saul, Brody and Mindy could find their specific parent.

Amelia gave Brody a bathroom break and a snack with a promise of helping them stretch before they headed out for their search.

Amelia sent Saul over to the swings and she joined him for a bit, making sure she set a time limit of 15 minutes. This day was starting out in good form. Each person had a little time to spend focusing on their strengths before they headed out for the search.

The search was going to entail having them work together and she needed them feeling like they were being heard. Investing in each one before the search helped Amelia as well. She was feeling very satisfied and looked forward to helping the three of them.

As they went out for the day on Saturday, the group went with the list Mindy came up with. The first thing on the list was a place Mindy thought was good for Brody. Amelia was glad Mindy put Brody first, especially since Brody was overlooked on many occasions.

Mindy's idea was to head over to the farmers market and luck had it that they were within walking distance to the entrance of the first of many vegetable stands. The first stand was a large display of various peppers, zucchini and squash. Brody began viewing the various people working and buying produce near the stand. Many of them seemed to be a bit more health conscious and Brody noticed the questions some were asking about how the vegetables were grown.

Mindy never thought about how it was grown and also gravitated towards the questions being asked. It was amazing to learn about the different soil and varieties of species that could be grown in the local area right near their home.

Saul was surprised that he was actually enjoying looking at fruits and vegetables. The various colors, shapes and sizes were quite eye catching and he too was interested in a more visual way.

Amelia embraced the fact that the group was interested and decided that getting some grocery shopping done served her as well. The group taste tested samples from different stands and managed to get some fresh honey from a farmer in the area. It was an enjoyable day with input from everyone on what was the best produce to buy. The group was having fun together even though they had no leads on finding their parent.

As the day wound down to late afternoon, Amelia helped remind them that sometimes things are out of their control. Focusing on the present moment can open them up to their intuition which can help unlock the memory of their parent.

Mindy was intrigued with this new bit of information. She wanted to know more about how she could be more present. Amelia immediately decided that they should spend the rest of the afternoon with no expectations, just see where the day took them.

Saul and Brody seemed open to that experience so they continued on sightseeing in the vicinity of the market with no particular demands of the group. Amelia helped them focus on their strengths, giving Mindy various moments to learn something new, having Saul wander around looking at whatever struck his fancy and making sure Brody got enough to eat and drink as the evening wore on.

It was one of those perfect days that everyone made the most of, including Amelia. They already were looking forward to more adventures with Amelia.

# CHAPTER 18

THE FOLLOWING DAY WAS SUNDAY. It was a day that started out raining pretty hard and Amelia was thinking she might not be totally on board with running but Brody, Saul and Mindy were ready waiting for her with their running gear on as she headed down their street.

She was energized by their enthusiasm and figured why rock the boat if things were going well. Still they hadn't had a glimpse of one parent but they were sharing more, they were starting to be more present and she was individually working with them to find their parent.

Amelia had been wanting to push the boundaries a bit more and run 10 miles today. The rain was making it hard for her to wrap her head around actually accomplishing this big task. She was however excited that she wasn't doing this big task alone. She had Mindy, Saul and Brody joining her and she took a moment to remember her own words of advice from yesterday, STAY PRESENT.

The run started out surprisingly well. Amelia made it a point to look around and point out things that would keep Saul interested. She checked in with Mindy at various moments to see how far they had run and that they were staying on the correct trail. She had Brody remind them when they needed to drink and use the bathroom. It was an uncomfortable rain but the group seemed focused and each were enjoying their responsibility. Amelia just needed to keep this momentum for 8 more miles.

The rain continued to downpour. As the adult in this run, Amelia realized she was overseeing their best interests. She tried to help motivate the group by telling them a joke which no one seemed to get but the minute she started to act silly, the group became more engaged. This surprised Amelia and she started to think about previous times when the group was equally engaged.

She remembered the day at the cave when everyone was happily exploring and another time when they were doing yoga loudly. She was staying present on this run and as a result she was getting more insight on how this group responded. This group was best described as loud, silly and explorers.

At some point in the run, Amelia realized she bit off more than everyone could handle. They were still 3 miles away from getting back to the car. Amelia was at her wits end and then she remembered that the group loved to be loud, silly and exploratory. So she harnessed the silly side of them and had them clap and sing at the top of their lungs as they ran and it started working. They had picked up their speed.

She then had them search for animals in the trees ahead and also for mysteriously looking fairy doors at the bottom of the trees. It didn't matter that they never came upon one on the last 3 miles back. They were too distracted to realize that they had run those last tough rain-soaked miles and were already back celebrating their tremendous accomplishment of 10 miles.

Amelia was encouraged by the group's effort and was feeling quite proud of each and every one of them. She encouraged them to get some rest and that she would be there tomorrow to pick them up for school in the morning.

# CHAPTER 19

MONDAY MORNING CAME ABRUPTLY and Amelia was surprised at how everything in her life was coming together, even for a Monday. She had been a hot mess these past few years and somehow through her running she had met some wonderful kids who were slowly bringing her back to her true self.

These kids required a lot of focus and attention and she somehow didn't really mind spending time with them. They were revealing many things and she was eager to see them succeed in their own lives.

She was still a bit dismayed over not having found their parent but Amelia stayed hopeful. She was trying to fill that void as best she could and they were starting to really trust her. When she dropped Brody, Saul and Mindy off at school, Amelia promised them that she would see them after and that today was a day for relaxation.

Amelia knew that they had inspired her longer runs and she was relying on them more and more. She was excited to bring out the best in them and in return they brought out the best in her.

Since she planned today as a day for relaxation, she figured in a little time alone without Mindy, Saul and Brody. Later on, she would pick them up from school and the rest of the day they would continue in that relaxing fashion.

Amelia headed over to Red Trail, the place where she first noticed Mindy, Saul and Brody and found an empty bench near the base of the trail. She took some time to close her eyes and tune out the rest of the world.

She was present to the whole quiet experience. She focused on her breath and slowly let go. Nothingness and the quietness of the experience was showing her how to listen; how to get in touch with her intuition.

As twenty minutes passed, Amelia came to the realization that at some point in her life she had lost herself just like Mindy, Saul and Brody had lost their parent and now she knew exactly where to locate their parent. She couldn't wait to pick them up from school and show them.

# CHAPTER 20

THE END of the school day happened quickly and Amelia was there just as she promised to pick up Mindy, Saul and Brody. Each of them ready and excited to see what kind of relaxing day Amelia had in store for them. Amelia knew now how to find each of their parents and she was ready to help them see it through.

She took them over to the nearby park where they had met at the swings and had each of them sit on the picnic table. Amelia had them close their eyes and each let go of trying to control anything, just be present in the quietness. She had them try out the 20 minute time period like she had done earlier at Red Trail on the bench. Mindy had a hard time at first not overthinking. Amelia calmly reminded Mindy that it was only 20 minutes that she didn't need to think. Saul kept asking what time it was and Amelia lovingly touched his shoulder and told him she would let him know when the time was up and Brody was trying to itch their nose every few seconds that Amelia happily reminded them that they could hold off for a bit and not scratch.

It took a concerted effort by the three of them to finally quiet themselves to a state of complete bliss. It was just a few minutes of the twenty minute session but enough for them to realize THE ANSWER.

\* \* \*

Mindy was the extension of Amelia's mind; a mind that could run off and keep her from her true self. A mind that needed the support of a body and soul to operate efficiently. A mind that could let go and not have to be in charge all the time.

Saul was the extension of Amelia's soul; a soul that was free to explore but needed time limits to be satisfied. A soul that wanted to be more than just unlimited freedom but to have structure to gain purpose.

Brody was the extension of Amelia's body; the driving force in keeping the mind and soul more regulated. A body that needed balance and was happiest when life was simple.

\* \* \*

For I am Amelia and Amelia is me. They weren't looking for their parent but I was looking for them. It took separating them out and realizing that they were childlike energies that needed parental guidance. I wasn't even aware of them in that detail until they showed up to me in a childlike way.

It's always interesting how when someone needs your help and you are able; you then spring into action helping them as best as you can but if you need help from yourself, it gets put on the back burner.

This was a tale of two tells: the parts inside that needed help and the fact that they are just extensions of you. It's much easier to help when you separate them out and I now do this all the time.

\* \* \*

By now you might have figured how my characters got into this story. Mindy is my mind, Saul is my soul and Brody is my body and they are my kids, or at least I treat them that way now that I have gotten to know them.

I am more compassionate, loving and kind to my kiddos and they in turn are excited to work together to help me succeed in life.

\* \* \*

For Mindy is the Why (**Y**) in my **mind**, Saul is the ahh (**A**) in my **soul** and Brody is the **Be Respectful** in my **body**. I need them to operate productively in this life of mine and I am so glad I found them and listened to them.

\* \* \*

As my favorite childhood book reminds me that it's not scary to find and discover you. You are NOT the monster at the end of this book. You don't need to be afraid of turning the page to discover your true identity. Your Mindy, Saul and Brody are waiting for you.

*NOW TURN THE PAGE!*

# THE SEARCH FOR YOU

Wow, what wonderful timing! You have turned the page and are finally ready to discover your Mindy, your Saul, and your Brody. This next section is your adventure.

-------------

Finding yourself may seem easy, given that we spend all day with ourselves, but it can actually be quite challenging. We rarely have time entirely to ourselves to truly get to know and discover who we are.

We enter this world and are immediately conditioned by others to talk, walk, learn, and explore based on their experiences. It's no wonder some of us take over 60 years to reach our authentic selves, and even then, we may still question if it truly is us.

This part of the book represents an adventure into the undiscovered crevices and cracks of your being. It's the process of unraveling you. This journey can be both scary and exhilarating. Be open and honest with yourself by committing to finishing this marathon of a book. It is when we take this commitment seriously that we can genuinely start to trust ourselves and desire to get to know YOU.

So, let's take stock of where you are at this very moment. Allow yourself to see the various selves within you, including those undiscovered ones. To do this, imagine something in your life that you are resisting.

Is it dating? Finding a new job? Organizing your home? Finishing a project? Everyone has something in their life that they resist. Take a moment and think about one of those things you are avoiding.

What internal dialogue is happening in your head? Does this exercise feel silly? Are you feeling anxious? Do you question why you bought this book? Are you thinking that there's no way it can get finished, fixed, or found?

All of these fleeting thoughts are significant, but for this exercise, I ask those parts of you that have started to chatter away in your mind to step outside yourself. Acknowledge those parts as important, thank them for their warnings, but kindly ask them to stay outside because you aren't entertaining those thoughts right now.

Once that is done, imagine the life experience you are resisting. Really visualize it and bring it to life! Imagine it. Each time something arises in your imagination that hinders your thought of achievement, thank that part of you and release it back out with the others from the beginning of the exercise, all while continuing to picture yourself engaging with what you're resisting.

When you reach your visualized goal, notice the beauty of it all and the accomplishment. If additional internal voices or naysayers arise, send them outside of your system. You want to keep only those parts of you that are excited and cheering you on.

Now, take a moment to observe the parts of you that are outside, the ones you removed from your system. Are there many or just a few? Each of these parts are important as well. Recognizing that we don't have everyone on board is the first step toward actualizing your authentic self.

Each of those parts outside needs your attention and understanding. They have been ignored and dismissed in the past, which is why they now attempt to sabotage you. You must begin to trust and listen to them.

These parts represent all the times you did not listen to or understand yourself. This is your first aha moment, a chance to allow the past to guide you and assist you in discovering your authentic self.

Trust that they aren't intentionally sabotaging you; they are merely untrusting and fearful. You will gain the tools in this book to help them and in return help yourself.

# MEET IN THE MIDDLE

Now, let's continue this adventure inward. Before any adventure, you need to know where you are going. Maybe not all the details, but at least the basic map so you know which direction you are headed.

So, let's locate your map. Generally, a map has coordinates for where you can begin and end at a particular destination. The best part of YOUR map is the middle. It doesn't matter where you start or where you end up; the good stuff is in the middle - the actual adventure.

The middle part is where we want to begin. Do you have a lot of mountainous difficulties on your map that keep you from your best life? Are you unfamiliar with finding a different way to get from point A to point B? Do you have many personal road hazards on your map?

There are various barriers we have put up over the years to keep us from trusting ourselves. This is where true change begins. Trust that you can do this. Trust that you don't want to let yourself down.

* * *

Take a minute to speak these affirmations into existence.

1. Tell yourself you are reading this section of the book because you are finally ready to trust yourself.

2. You are open to working with yourself to get your mind, body, and soul on the same page.

3. You no longer want to compete with yourself.

4. There is no reason anymore to sabotage yourself.

5. You are open to the process of really getting to know yourself by being honest and not judging.

* * *

Acknowledgment of this is especially important if you are genuinely going to reach your authentic self. So, truly start to believe that you want to affirm the above statements. You may have to recite them a few times and if at all possible in front of a mirror.

Repetition is helpful for remembering and reminding you that you are important. It also helps as we introduce you to your mind, body, and soul all over again.

Remember, this is an adventure. So have some fun getting to know the middle part of your map. It's where all the memories are created and where the juicy stories are found.

# THE RIGHT NOW

WHAT IF THE greatest adventure of your life wasn't waiting somewhere far ahead, but already unfolding around you, within you, *right now*?

We often wait for a signal, a big moment, a milestone or something that says, *Now you may begin.*

You are already in the middle. You've been on the journey all along. Every breath you're taking is the awareness rising in you. It is the invitation to go deeper.

We look for maps in other people. We spend much of our lives copying, mimicking, and following what "worked" for someone else. We collect blueprints and strategies, hoping one will fit. But the real map is made for you and by you through *discovery*, not duplication.

Right now, you can begin to chart your course differently, not because something is broken, but because something new is awakening.

You're not here to become a better copy of someone else. You're here to remember what's *original* in you. You are here to trace your own wonder and to listen to the inner compass that never stopped humming, even when the noise of the world drowned it out.

If you're feeling the nudge to see things differently, that's all the readiness you need. Because what if the goal was never to *get somewhere* but to become someone more *true*?

* * *

Much of what we think of "us" is borrowed.

1. The way we speak.

2. The way we people-please.

3. The way we try to earn love.

4. The masks.

5. The expectations.

6. The versions we play.

But now, you're invited to undo all of that. You are here reading this book to peel back the layers of conditioning and to feel into your *real* answers, your *real* rhythm, and your *real* needs. This undoing isn't destruction, it's liberation. It's like finding a hidden trail under your feet that's been waiting for you to notice.

# PARENTING

WE ARE REALLY TAUGHT the backwards way when it comes to parenting. Parenting, we're told, is about teaching, correcting, disciplining, shaping. It's about rules and rewards. About keeping things under control.

Most of us were raised in a world of external parenting.

Do this. Don't do that. Be this. Don't be that.

You're too loud. You're too quiet. You're too much. You're not enough.

So, we grew up trying to parent ourselves through shame, through judgment, and through "shoulds." When that didn't work, we turned that same model outward trying to manage everyone else's behavior so we could feel safe inside.

Parenting isn't something you do to others. It's something you do within. True parenting is learning how to hold yourself. It is setting boundaries not as punishment, but as protection.

It is compromising not by giving yourself away, but by honoring every voice within you.

Parenting is to listen not to the loudest fear, but to the softest truth. It's not about making yourself behave. It's about creating a safe, loving environment within you so that you *want* to show up differently.

* * *

This is how you re-parent yourself:

With gentleness

With courage

With honesty

With trust

Through parenting, you can rediscover how you will need to approach your mind, your body and your soul.

# THE CHILDREN WITHIN

INSIDE YOU LIVE three powerful children:

Your **Mind**.

Your **Body**.

Your **Soul**.

Each one has its own language, its own needs, its own wisdom and above them all, guiding them gently, patiently, wisely... is your **Higher Self**—the true Parent within you.

When you begin to see yourself this way, everything changes. You stop pushing. You start listening. You stop fighting yourself. You start uniting yourself.

Each child brings a gift. When you stop making any of them "wrong," you can begin to optimize their strengths. You delegate. You trust. This is where the magic starts to happen.

So TURN THE PAGE to meet these wonderful children within.

# MIND

THE FIRST CHILD of yours is your **mind**. The mind is there to complete tasks, learn and stabilize. This child should not be involved in the decision making of your life. It is only a child and should not have that much responsibility. You might be realizing at this moment that you have left your mind in charge more than you should in the past. This is ok. You are finally realizing the reasons why things have not gone as well in your life as they could.

The mind is best served when you *give it tasks*, such as laundry, loading the dishwasher, and paying bills. The mind should not be deciding what to wear, what meal to eat and what you should spend your money on. This will be handled by you as a whole when you finally figure out what each child can do.

Along with tasks, give your mind *something to learn*. At a certain point in your life the learning seems to slow down and the tasks get larger and larger. Take this time to start to rectify that imbalance by learning something new. Your parent self, which is just your higher self, knows what you want to learn. Maybe, it is something you have been avoiding because you think it may be too hard to learn at this time. Maybe, it is something that costs money you don't have. Maybe, you have come up with too many excuses to not learn something new but your higher self knows. So, try to learn something new. Take a class. Learn a new language. Try to learn that dance step. Learn a new technique of something you have already mastered. Learning keeps the mind in a happy place. No child wants to do tasks all the time, even your mind, so add learning something on a consistent basis to helping that child prosper.

There is one part of your mind that we need to be truly aware of: gossip. Your mind loves gossip which is why you need to constantly *stabilize*. Stabilizing means the mind is unlikely to give way once you give it information. This is how your mind carries out tasks and learns but it is also how and why the mind has a hard time changing.

So give it information but be careful what information you give your mind because it is very hard to overturn. This is the gossip. These are the stories you tell yourself over and over that keep you from your authenticity. It might be the story that you are not good enough, it might be that you talk yourself out of things that you want, all of it is gossip.

If you aren't learning, doing tasks and stabilizing, you are feeding into your own gossip. So be careful of your own internal dialogue and be compassionate with your mind.

# BODY

YOUR NEXT CHILD is your *body*. The body needs only *nourishment, movement* and *sleep*. This is literally your most basic child. It wants boring. When you are trying to figure out what each child needs in later chapters, this child is the child that is very vanilla. So, allow that child to be basic. It has a lot of responsibility just functioning every day for you, so basic is how you keep this child balanced.

Don't push too much when you are doing something for the body. Really listen. Just try going to the bathroom when your body tells you. Just like when a child needs to go pee, you would automatically go and find a bathroom, do the same for yourself. The same goes for thirst. If you are thirsty, make a point to go get something to drink. Don't force extra water to get a certain amount per day, your body doesn't work like that and you aren't listening.

This child is not prepared to diet, this tidbit of information many of us generally get wrong. Dieting is gossip from the last chapter. This means child mind is in charge of your body when it comes to dieting. Now think of that for a minute. One child telling another child what to do for days at a time. It might go well for a few days but it won't last. That child is going to finally have a tantrum and it won't be pretty. Take this time now to start to reassess how you nourish your body. Your body just wants *basic nourishment*, nothing fancy, nothing too complicated.

Your body also doesn't want to sit idly. It loves to move but recognize that it wants to *move* without the forceful presence of the mind. Being careful not to have your child mind deciding how much movement your body should do can prevent major problems or possibly catastrophic situations in your life.

Movement, basic movement, just a walk around the block everyday can be just the trick. The body is happy when you move your muscles, just like children, it is torture to sit all day, so take breaks in your day to just move.

Your child body must have *sleep* to really work. A tired child is the worst. They tend to throw the whole day off kilt. The other 2 children absorb the drama of the tired body and it reflects in the chaos of the day. So, try to make a point to put your body to bed at a decent time. Your parent self should really make an effort in this area. Find the right bedtime that works for you and stick to it.

This basic child needs consistency. The more consistent you get with this the better your body will respond.

So, if your body needs at least 7 hours of sleep, find the right time to put your body to bed and try to stick to it as best as you can. Keep the two-hour rule of sleep if at all possible, it will do wonders.

This means if your bedtime is 10 p.m., try staying within two hours of that time. Don't go to bed before 8 p.m. or after 12 a.m.

This is also true for the awakening time. If you get up normally at 7 a.m., keep to the 2-hour rule as well and try your best not to sleep past 9 a.m. on a day you don't have to keep time. This is extremely important to maintaining a lifelong content body.

# SOUL

THE FINAL CHILD is your *soul*. This child's main response is joy. This child only wants to do joyful things, things that make them happy or content. This part wants *creativity, variety and fun*. This child is not interested in working hard just having fun. The soul is the nonconforming child. It is a shower with no soap, a walk with no place in mind, playing in the sand, a no desired outcome.

This one doesn't know the difference between one hour and one minute. It's one of the things that is fascinating about this child but also can be the most infuriating part too. The soul is good at delaying and keeping everything in a time warp.

This is a perfect time to recall an annual story about the children at my community pool having fun swimming and playing in the water and their parents telling them that they need to get out of the pool in 5 minutes. Just like the soul, these children go on playing for another 30 minutes until their parent reminds them again and they continue to play in the water until it becomes more like 45 minutes and then they finally force them out of the water. It's the parents influence that finally gets them to take action.

The soul needs the parent/higher self. This is the way you set time limits. When you know that this child is not good at keeping time, why would you let it figure out when to get out of the water. Parenting this child to delicately work in joy on your time frame and being careful not to lose track in it will be important.

# SABOTEURS

NOW THAT YOU understand you have your own inner children—your mind, body, and soul—it's time to look at what they've been carrying.

To move forward in wholeness, we must begin the process of deconstructing past emotional experiences. Over the years, parts of you have taken on roles as saboteurs—not because they are bad, but because they were trying to protect you. These are wounded aspects of your mind, body, or soul, wrapped tightly in old feelings and unhealed moments.

These saboteurs don't announce themselves clearly. They're tangled in emotion, confusion, and past pain.

It's not always obvious which part of you is speaking, or where the reaction is coming from. That's okay. You're not here to analyze or judge. You're here to listen and reconnect.

You've now learned who your inner children truly are and what each represents.

As you begin to build trust within yourself again, your first step is honoring your feelings. Emotions are not problems to fix. They are signals. They are valid. They are sacred. And they are never "wrong."Emotions are *not* rational because they're not meant to be. They're meant to be felt, not ranked.

\* \* \*

One emotion is not more valuable than another.

- Sadness is just as worthy as happiness.
- Fear is just as important as excitement.
- Grief, joy, anger, peace—all of them are part of your guidance system.

\* \* \*

When you give yourself full permission to feel without labeling, you open the door to deep healing. That's how you begin to untangle the confusion and hear each child clearly. That's how you start to parent your inner world with compassion and clarity.

This is where integration begins and from here, real transformation unfolds.

\* \* \*

As things happen in your life, many of us do not process our emotions. We instead bottle them up like time capsules. They are emotions that we connected through life experiences. Many do not even reveal what actually occurred but they are important because we haven't processed them.

These emotions haven't gone away. They are still stuck and stored somewhere inside your body. Those parts have been bottled up and still remain in the energy of your past. Some might be thinking it's August 1, 2009, other parts might think it was last year. They may not even make sense. But each experience has become a time capsule of sorts because you have ignored them and not honored their experience and sacrifice. This time capsule creates enemies of yourself. This is the part that sabotages.

How do you know that you have saboteurs? It's easy. It's the parts of you that are not accountable or are too accountable.

I like to use the 3-day rule. Are you on day 3 of doing anything the same? Not showering for 3 days, obsessing over something for the 3rd day, day 3 of eating chips, 3 days of staying up late, 3 days straight working out, 3 days of travel with no rest, 3 days of painting, 3 days of drinking, day 3 of not leaving your house.

When you find yourself on day three, that is when you need to take some time to connect with yourself through the following exercise.

# RELEASING EMOTIONAL
# TIME BOMBS

TAKE A FEW DEEP BREATHS. Remind yourself to stay as the adult. Now focus on keeping your heart open and give your adult self a big hug. Bring your energy and focus down to your gut and send unconditional love to those parts of you that you have put in the emotional time capsules, you don't need to know what they are but many times you can feel the emotion. This is the places of darkness inside of you.

Welcome them into this exercise and tell them that it is safe to come out into the open. While you are not perfect or healed, you are in a safer situation at the present time. You may at this time sense one or more stuck parts of you coming out into your field of vision or the emotion of it.

Continue to send a gentle loving welcome. Tell those emotional entities that you love them. Tell them that you are sorry that you have ignored them but that now you are coming back for them and that you need them in your life. Thank them for going through what they went through and really feel the emotion.

You don't need to replay the past just help those parts of you feel through it by giving them imaginary hugs and imagine doing something with them that you like to do. You of course, know what makes you feel safe, so do something safe with them. Create a new memory with your parent self, empowering your time-capsule versions of you.

Ask if they want to merge and join you as a parent in the present day. Explain to them that they can experience a life full of freedom and decisions coming from your current self. Take this time to imagine those past parts of you growing up before your eyes to your current present day self.

Feel them merge and become part of you. See the years of the past release and feel your parent/higher self getting stronger.

If you still feel emotions hanging around after you allowed those parts to merge, that is your clue that there is one or more versions of your past that don't want to merge. They are too broken or are still having a hard time trusting you. Tell them it's ok they don't have to merge but they too can finally be free of the emotion.

We can't fix everything in life and that includes your past but we can release it. That is when you truly start to love yourself.

Take this time to come up with an experience that would entice those broken parts to release from your internal system, your energy space. It might mean you imagine a rocket ship coming for that part of you to take you out of your system and blasting it off to another place. It might take a unicorn or dragon to get this part of you to leave.

Take some time thinking of things and offering your internal saboteurs this magical way of leaving your system. It may sound a bit corny, but this exercise really does work.

Many times we just needed an acknowledgment that that part of your life sucked and now we can imagine a great escape via a dragon. For me, it worked when I finally imagined a 100-person marching band with a red carpet helping to guide and release those broken parts.

This exercise will be important throughout the rest of your life. You will come back to it when you start noticing your life being sabotaged again. Remind yourself of the 3-day rule as it is always best when you can address your saboteur quickly.

You will find that the sooner you catch yourself, the more complete your life will be. I am still using this exercise on myself and it gets easier to merge and release the more you do it.

# 3-DAY RULE

WHEN YOU ACCESS YOUR EMOTIONS, you can start to completely understand your mind, body and soul. This is an ongoing thing. You are not automatically healed. This is a process you're going to have to look at and do for the rest of your life.

You're always evolving and you're always having triggers and emotional clumps of different things that happen to you that you don't take the time to deal with. So, every time you get outside of yourself and you put the blinders on or your earplugs on your inner voice, more and more time capsules or blocks start happening.

So, I like to look at always paying attention to the 3-day rule. Are you doing things to sabotage your life repeatedly beyond 3 days? Are you on day 3 of eating chips or crappy food? Chips are wonderful, by the way, but a lot of them is probably not good.

Or are you the person who hasn't showered, and it's now day 3? This is those kinds of moments where you say, "Hmm, I have a saboteur and I need to address it". It could be part of the mind, the body or soul, or different sections of your mind, body and soul that weren't listened to.

You had a big project and you ignored that you were hungry not once, not twice, but three times. In the process, you also knew that you had to use the restroom, but you kept holding going to the bathroom. That energy gets stored in your system as a part of you that doesn't trust you to listen to your inner cues.

Over time, it becomes some sort of blockage and it can lead to actually having physical problems. Some of the things that you've got going on in your knees, ankles, shoulders and hips, are lot of times where we've ignored our inner cue.

To keep ourselves at our optimal self, we need to start to pay attention. Did you go to day 3 where you didn't listen and make yourself accountable? Did you go to day 3 where you didn't acknowledge that you screwed up? This is when you need to get back to that exercise of **releasing your emotional time bombs**. You might even do that more frequently and be surprised at just taking that time out to say you're sorry and to listen and hear what you have to say to yourself can be very therapeutic.

*** 

*CONSISTENCY*

*YOU ARE MAKING TIME FOR YOURSELF*

***

# INTEGRATING THE
# PARTS OF YOU

DISCOVERING yourself is easy when you separate the parts of you and look at them individually. The real magic happens when you take those parts and integrate. It can be challenging if you do it in a manner that is not cohesive and loving. This exercise will help facilitate the merging of the mind, body and soul.

\* \* \*

Imagine a quiet theater with velvet seats and a single spotlight. You sit in the front row not as the critic, but as the Parent, the witness.

The stage belongs to your children now: your Mind, your Body, and your Soul.

Each one has a role to play. Each one has something to express and you are here to observe with love.

Before anything begins, invite all three of your inner children, the Mind, Body, and Soul to step behind the red curtain.

Now, take a deep breath. You are the Parent now, the one who sees the whole picture and the one who listens with compassion and never judges.

Gently call your Mind to center stage.

Watch it step out from behind the curtain.

Maybe it's a little nervous. Maybe it rushes forward with excitement. Maybe it hesitates.

This is your Mind—the planner, the protector, the problem-solver. It is strong. Capable. Sharp. And often... overworked.

Now pause. Really observe.

How does your Mind feel standing there in the light? Is it scared? Is it exhilarated? Is it unsure of its worth?

Now send your mind loving thoughts. Applaud your Mind. Thank it for its brilliance. Honor its vigilance. Celebrate its creativity.

Take a moment to watch and feel what happens.As the applause washes over it, the Mind might soften. It might stand taller. Smile wider. It begins to trust. It begins to breathe.

Ask it:

*What can you accomplish when you are loved instead of judged?*

And wait for the answer. Give your mind this moment and then watch and see it go off stage.

\* \* \*

Now, let your Body take center stage.

It steps out perhaps cautiously, perhaps confidently. It has carried so much. It holds your history, your instincts, your pain, and your pleasure.

Look at it with love. How does your Body feel being seen like this? Is it tired? Proud? Ashamed? Grateful?

Now give it the same applause. Loud and steady. Thank it for surviving and for moving.

Watch it relax. Maybe the shoulders drop. Maybe it dances. Maybe it weeps. Your Body is more than a vessel, it is sacred.

Ask it:

*What do you need to feel safe and honored?*

Listen with your whole being. Let the body have its moment and see it also go off stage.

* * *

Finally, invite your Soul to the stage.

It may float, glide, or move slowly with deep presence. Your Soul is ancient, knowing, eternal. It holds your truth and your calling.

How does your Soul feel being seen? Is it serene? Is it tender? Is it bold?

Applaud now—not loudly, but reverently. This is the applause of awe.

Witness it fully.

Ask it:

*What are you here to guide me toward?*

Take this instance to be still. Allow the Soul to have its moment.

\* \* \*

Now, bring them all back to center stage.

Mind. Body. Soul.

Imagine them forming a circle—facing one another, holding hands, breathing together.

Each one is *necessary*.

Each one is *powerful*.

Each one is *not complete without the others*.

Observe the energy between them.

Which one feels quiet now? Which one is reclaiming its voice? Is one leading? Is one learning to let go?

Now speak to them, as the Parent:

"I see you. I honor you. You are each vital. From now on, we work together. I will listen to all of you. We are no longer fragments. We are whole. We are one."

Let that moment settle. Let the integration warm you. Take one final breath and welcome them back into your being.

Mind. Body. Soul.

Aligned. United. Empowered.

Feel the strength. Feel the connection. Feel the deep, quiet knowing that you are now ready to lead with love, not control. You are no longer just reacting to life. You are conducting it.

# WANT TO, HAVE TO, FORCED TO

IT'S easy to merge your mind, body, and soul when you *want to* do something. So, when I want to do something, it seems to be most parts of myself are on board. I want to go to the movies. My mind researches the movie, my body feels like, oh yeah, I just want to sit and do nothing. My soul is like, yes, this is a new movie that's coming out. It sure seems a lot easier to integrate that mind, body and soul when do you *want to* do something.

But there's two other sections of your life where you *have to* actually do something that you don't want to do. This is when things get a little more tricky.

There are three ways of looking at things in your life. You *want to*, which means it's kind of an easier way to get those three children of yours on board; you *have to* and that means, well, you kind of *have to* do this. You know, you have to get up and take a shower and go to work, okay? So, this is reflective of the things that get you through the day to day stuff. You *have to* because you're required to pay the bills, so you got to go to work.

Some days you don't feel like it. So how do you get your mind wrapped around that? How do you get your soul that just wants to go and fluff off and go to the movies? How do you get that part to do some work? This is when things get a little bit more cumbersome.

And finally, the biggest one is when you're *forced to*. That's the hardest one. That's where you have to be the parent and be really careful on how you approach being *forced to* do something.

Forced to situations could be going to a wedding that you don't like one of the people or it is a funeral of a particular individual that maybe it's going to unearth some old feelings about other family members. This is the *force to* situation. This is where you need to be a even more careful with your parts.

You are forced to find ways to set boundaries and create a safe space for your mind, your body and soul. And so this chapter is to reflect that. Make sure those *forced to* events, especially those ones, that you take some time and really check in.

What can do for your mind if you are forced to go to a funeral? Your mind could plan something near the funeral. and it could do a bunch of research about that.

For instance, you could figure out where you would want to eat before or after the funeral, Or it could be completing something that you've been wanting to gift somebody at that funeral. Maybe the funeral's not the thing, but maybe it's the completion of something that you can learn, create, and do for someone else.

And then maybe for the body, it's just seeing the stress that incurs, maybe realizing that your body can only handle so much stress. So you're going to limit your time.

Maybe you're going to get there a little late, so people don't have that much time to talk to you before the actual service, or maybe use the bathroom excuse. Always listening and asking the mind, body and soul what it needs to get through that *forced to* event.

Taking time during that *forced to* event to listen to that body. You need to go to the bathroom and getting up and going to the bathroom helps your body destress from the *forced to* situation.

For your soul, in order to handle the *forced to* situation, maybe it's just wearing something deceitful. Maybe that person wouldn't have approved of red underwear or a tattoo. Maybe you even put a bunch of fake tattoos on your body and go into that funeral wearing them.

Your soul will get a kick out of that and know that secretly you are enjoying and having played a role of wearing tattoos to this funeral, which would be very disapproving for that person. Look at ways you can kind of cajole those parts. This is very offbeat, but it works. I have found that that it kind of desensitizes you and calms you.

Many times, it makes you look forward to the event a little more due to your devious plans that are not devious at all. It's just more internal humor or internal jokes. Internal jokes are always the best when only you know it's funny. So, keep those to a minimum with yourself.

Don't tell other people and really listen to those *forced to* moments. This is where the connection of mind, body, and soul, alignment starts to come into play; when you *want to* do something, when you *have to* do something, and when you're *forced to* do something.

\* \* \*

### *IT'S NOT SPIRITUAL TO HOLD YOUR PEE*

\* \* \*

# SPEAKING YOUR TRUTH

YOU ARE DOING THE WORK. Your Mind, Body, and Soul—the children within—have stepped forward, been seen, honored, and united. You've listened. You've held space. You've allowed healing to begin.

So now, it's time to let go. Seriously... let go. Stop trying to rein them in. Stop micromanaging their every move. They are not wild animals to tame. They are now a team—your team—and they're ready to breathe, grow, and soar. Let them be free.

Integration doesn't mean control. It means unity, trust, and aligned purpose. You are no longer split into parts fighting for dominance. You are whole. So let your team stretch their legs and live.

Whatever is left causing friction, self-doubt, or anxiety isn't your team. It's residue. It's the leftover noise. It's old expectations, unspoken truths, copied behaviors and borrowed identities.

This is the time to take a deep breath and ask:

"What in me is still pretending?"

"What am I doing that's not me?"

You were never meant to be a copy. You came here to be original. Your soul was never designed to be a replica of someone else's path.

But when you don't speak your truth, and suppress that deep knowing, you start to fracture again. You make room for chaos.

Think about a time when you didn't speak your truth; that relationship you stayed in too long; that job you knew wasn't right; that trip you said yes to even though your gut screamed "no." What happened?

Chances are, it complicated your life in ways you didn't expect. You may have gotten sick. Or felt depressed. Or drifted far off course from where you truly wanted to be. That wasn't just "a bad decision." That was you ignoring the voice of your team.

You know the voice. The one that shouts in silence. The one that burns in your gut when something is *off*. That's your truth. We've all had those moments where our entire insides scream for us to do something different—to speak up, to walk away, to choose ourselves.

The question is… did you listen? Or did you override it to keep the peace, avoid discomfort, or stay in control?

Your inner voice is a compilation of your mind, body and soul. The more you start honoring that voice, the stronger it gets. And the more intuitive, clear, and simple your life becomes.

Now that you've aligned your inner team, their voice will become louder and harder to ignore.

This is a blessing—but it's also a responsibility. If you ignore them now, they won't go quiet. They'll revolt. Your Body may get sick. Your Mind may spiral into anxiety or overthinking. Your Soul may go numb.

Don't silence your team. Don't compete with them. Lead with them. This moment—right now—is where the rubber meets the road. Where this internal unity starts showing up in your external world.

In your relationships, if something feels out of sync, it likely is. Maybe your Mind is saying "this makes sense," but your Body is tense. Maybe your Soul is whispering, "this is not it," but you're ignoring it to avoid conflict. That's a red flag.

Each child has their own experience, and each deserves a voice. Try not to let your Mind decide what the Body needs. Don't let your Soul's truth get buried under practicality. Your job now is to keep listening, keep aligning, and keep choosing what's real not what is rehearsed.

You are building a relationship with your self that is honest, integrated, and awake. But integration isn't the end. It's the beginning. It's the invitation to become **Authentically You!**

So now, the real adventure begins:

- Let go.
- Trust your team.
- Speak your truth.
- Live from the inside out.

And remember: You were never broken. You were just divided. Now, you are whole.

And that wholeness is your new freedom.

# THE POWER OF STILLNESS

SOME DAYS, no matter how far you've come, no matter how much you've grown or how aligned your inner team feels, everything falls apart. Your Mind starts racing. Your Body aches, fidgets, or flat-out resists. Your Soul feels distant or over-emotional or heavy. And you—the parent of them all—sit there wondering how the heck you're supposed to bring them back together.

This is not failure. This is just life and more importantly, this is your cue to stop trying.

To stop fixing and to call a time-out. Sometimes the most powerful parenting move is not to figure anything out. Sometimes, it's simply to pause. And not in a cozy, pampered, scented-bath sort of way. We're talking about raw stillness. No music. No tea. No essential oils or fuzzy blankets.

Just you. A chair. Silence. Taking a true time-out.

1. Find a place that's neutral—not comforting, not uncomfortable, just still.
2. Sit down. Eyes closed. Back straight if you can.
3. Set a timer for 20 minutes, preferably not from your phone.
4. And then... just be.

If your Mind starts to wander, plan or fix; say gently, but firmly: "No. Be quiet now." just like you would a talkative child at bedtime.

If your Body gets twitchy with an itch here, a cramp there, or a full-on tantrum to get up; tell it: "We're not doing that right now. I'll deal with you in 20 minutes."

If your Soul begins to stir with emotion such as sadness, longing, or boredom; whisper: "I hear you. But now is not the time. Just be with me."

Stillness is not inactivity, it's a deep presence. When you allow your whole system to stop, without escape or stimulation, you give yourself the sacred space to reboot.

Think of it like putting all your children in the same quiet room, telling them not to speak, and simply letting them sit. Not because they're in trouble, but because they need to recalibrate. After a while, things settle. The noise inside dies down and what's real begins to rise. Sometimes, that 20 minutes is all it takes to come back with clarity.

Being the parent of your internal team doesn't mean you always know what to do. In fact, the best parents know when to say: "I don't know what to do right now. So, let's just be quiet together.

” That's the kind of leadership that builds trust with your Mind, your Body, your Soul and most of all, with you.

*** *** ***

*LOVE*

*YOU LOVE WHAT YOU ARE DISCOVERING*

*** *** ***

# WHAT'S AT YOUR CORE

I OFTEN THINK that the most influential part to becoming your authentic self is to uncover your core being. Words that describe who you are at your core. I am silly, yes, silly. It can be annoying to many but I find my silliness hilarious and really love that I am silly.

It wasn't until someone in my past thought my silliness was stupid that I realized that it was my core word. It was something about me that I was unwilling to budge. I was unwilling to change that part of me so I let go of that person.

I want to be silly even when others don't want me to be. So, I have people in my life that like my silliness or at least tolerate my silliness and don't try to change that about me.

Think about your core words that best describe you. Remember these words cannot describe what you are to others. Yes, you might be a sister, a brother, a father, a nurse, but that does not describe who you are individually. Choose three to five words and make it a point to ask yourself if it is a word that you cannot budge on. If your answer is yes, then that is one of your core words.

Another one of my core words is loud. I am loud and it is something I don't want to change about me. I love that I am loud. Now, I recognize that sometimes I can't be loud and those are rare times. But if someone is trying to shush me when I am in an appropriate place where I can be loud, that is when I am triggered. I don't like it because I am not willing to budge and that is ok. It is my core word. It's such a core word that I didn't even realize that I named this subject and trademarked it with an exclamation point. Authentically You! ®. Someone pointed that out in one my classes and I realized my parent self knew all along that loud was one of my core words. Hilarious!

My last core word is exploratory. Yes, exploratory. It sounds weird but when I checked in with my mind, body and soul that is what they came up with. I am not nosey. I don't need to know everything. I just need to explore every day. It can be on walks, in a building or even in a box of miscellaneous items. The exploratory phase is what I cherish the most not the answer. It took me a while to figure that one out and that may be the case for you on one of your words.

The words need to reflect what all parts of you want. Each child needs to be in agreement. So maybe just looking up the thesaurus of a word you like can help your children rally around one particular word.

The intention of making this list is to decide what words best describe you that you cannot live without. For example, a person may be organized and love organization but it is not an absolute to their whole being that their life be organized at all times. This word: organized, would not be a core word.

However, this same person is also curious and it would be detrimental if they could not ask questions to others. Their curiousness is a core word because they need to be curious in order to be their true self.

Choose those words based on if you were asked to not have that word be your identity for a week you would not be ok. If you can answer that you would be ok that you could not identify yourself with that description of you for a week, then it is not your core word.

Core words are never bad. For example, one of my best friend's core words is selfish. I love this about her. She always makes sure she is fed, dressed and housed first and foremost. This is fabulous for me because I don't have to worry about whether or not her needs are being met. She has many wonderful facets and selfish energy is never bad when the people around you embrace it. Her other core word is planner, which I got to say is a tremendous bonus when you want to travel.

We have many facets of ourself which round us out, but our core words are a deal breaker. Can you start to see people in your life or places of jobs that don't fit in with your core words? Maybe it truly is time to make a change, specifically if you have a need to try to alter your core words. When it comes to new jobs and relationships, make sure you don't forget about those core words. That is what makes you unique. That is what makes you an original.

# PITFALLS

BECOMING AUTHENTICALLY YOU! sounds freeing but the journey is not without its challenges. Many people expect that once they commit to living their truth, the path will unfold effortlessly. But in reality, choosing to live authentically is choosing to live bravely and with that comes resistance, old patterns, and unexpected detours.

That's why we need to explore the common pitfalls, so you're not blindsided. This will help empower you to keep going.

\* \* \*

### The Approval Trap

One of the first traps we fall into is seeking validation. You may start expressing your truth, only to notice you're still subtly curating it for applause. You might think, "If they approve of this version of me, I must be doing it right." but authenticity isn't a performance.

**Warning sign:** You feel drained after being around certain people, despite "being yourself."

**Practice instead:** Ask yourself, "Am I saying this because it's true for me, or because I think they'll like it?" Let truth, not applause, guide your voice.

*  *  *

### The Ghosts of Old Beliefs

Even as you declare your freedom, the old voices return. "You're too much." "You're not enough." "Don't rock the boat." These whispers were planted long ago—by family, culture, religion, or fear. And when you're tired or vulnerable, they resurface.

**Warning sign:** You find yourself shrinking in the moments you most need to expand.

**Practice instead:** Say out loud: "I forgive all my old thoughts. I release them. They are not me anymore." Then breathe that freedom into your heart.

*  *  *

### Overcompensating with Force

Once people begin stepping into their truth, they often swing hard the other way. They start overstating who they are, using volume instead of vibration. This is common when we're still scared we won't be accepted.

**Warning sign:** You feel the need to convince others of your worth or identity.

**Practice instead:** Let your presence speak. Soft power is still power. True authenticity is like a mountain, it doesn't need to explain itself.

### Loneliness on the Path

Sometimes being authentic feels lonely. You start to see through dynamics that no longer serve you. You realize certain relationships were built on roles, not realness. And when you step out of those roles, people may leave.

**Warning sign:** You miss the "comfort" of being who others needed you to be.

**Practice instead:** Mourn the loss and enjoy the space you've created. That space is and will be filled with real connection, honest love, and mutual respect.

### Spiritual Bypass and Escaping Reality

In your desire to stay authentic, you may start avoiding difficult emotions or uncomfortable truths. But ignoring your pain doesn't make you more enlightened. It makes you disconnected from your humanity, and from others.

**Warning sign:** You catch yourself saying "It's all good" when it's not.

**Practice instead:** Sit with what hurts and breathe into it. Your parts don't need protection from the truth, they need permission to feel.

## *The Fear of Being Seen*

When you show up as the real you, there's nowhere to hide. That can feel terrifying. Vulnerability is often mistaken for weakness, but it is the birthplace of power. Being seen can be the hardest thing you do.

**Warning sign:** You delay launching the project, avoid the mirror, or distract yourself with busyness.

**Practice instead:** Whisper, "I believe I am good enough right now, at this very moment." Then look yourself in the eye. That person is worth being seen.

\* \* \*

Every time you choose truth over habit, love over fear, and presence over performance, you move closer to your divine center. Yes, the path to being Authentically You! has pitfalls. But each one is an invitation to deepen your roots.

*\* \* \**

*TRUST*

*YOU ACKNOWLEDGE AND LISTEN TO YOUR MIND,
BODY AND SOUL*

*\* \* \**

# FORGIVENESS

FORGIVENESS IS NOT A ONE-TIME ACT. It is a process of release and renewal. We carry so many beliefs, identities, and expectations shaped by the thoughts of others and the echoes of our past. What happens when we choose to let it all go?

Today, I choose to forgive everyone I believed in my past, not because they asked for it, not because they deserve it, but because I deserve peace. I forgive the roles they played in my story. I forgive the mirrors, the messengers and the mistaken heroes. I release their influence and reclaim my power.

I forgive the thoughts that once kept me small. The ones that whispered, *You're not enough. You're too much. You should be someone else.* Those were never mine to begin with. I release them with love and gratitude, for they showed me what no longer serves my soul.

In this space of release, I come home to myself. I love each part of who I am—my brilliant mind, my resilient body, and my infinite soul. I do not need to become something else to be worthy. I believe I am good enough right now, in this very moment. There is nothing missing. Nothing broken. Nothing wrong.

All is perfect, whole, and complete.

It is safe now. Safe to love my past self who was learning. Safe to love my current self who is growing. Safe to love my future self who is already blooming.

Forgiveness unlocks the heart. It calls in the divine.

I invite my higher self to continue the sacred overhaul of my belief system, stripping away fear, scarcity, and shame—until only love remains. And in that love, I rise. I walk differently. I speak with clarity. I no longer beg for validation, because I know: **I am truly loved at all times.**

I see only the loving self in me. And all others are gently released.

This is my freedom. This is my truth. This is forgiveness in its most sacred form.

# STEPPING INTO YOUR POWER

*LET GO of the need to have, be or do something.* That belief holds us back and keeps us out of our own power. These are external decisions and are not in the best interest of your children: your mind, body and soul.

Ask your mind, body and soul if they are onboard with any decision you make. This is how you start to learn what you really need. You probably don't ask yourself enough questions and really listen to the answers. Over time, you will feel intuitively guided and you won't have to literally ask them each time you do something.

You will feel a sense of joy because you are getting in alignment and stepping into your power. It takes some time to understand your children (mind, body and soul). They are still handicapped by the past and it will take some time, trust and love.

### 3 Key Questions to Stay in your Power

1. HOW MUCH TIME DO THEY NEED? – Are you allowing for too much time or not enough time to do something for your mind, body and soul?

The days of working all day and focusing on the rest and relaxation on the weekend, is over. Make time each day to work, play and take care of your body. Try to at least give a full 15 minutes to each of your parts. Make a wholesome breakfast. Take a shower with no soap and just relax. Check one thing off your list instead of all the things on your list. Try to at least balance the day out. If you are unable, try to spend those 15 minutes at least on the part you ignored that day.

2. DOES THE IDEA NEED TO BE ALTERED BASED ON TRUST? - Did you overpromise yourself something that in no way, shape or form is going to happen.

Catch yourself as soon as you get to a point in the day where you unable to fulfill what you promised yourself. Tell yourself you are sorry and ask yourself what would be ok to actually do with the remaining time you have of the day. You will be surprised how well your life will go by altering and accepting when you overpromise.

3. WILL YOU FOCUS ON THE LOVE FOR YOUR CHILDREN WHEN THEY ARE REBELLING?

Try to not get so down on yourself or angry when things don't go as planned. Life is going to always throw you curveballs, so give yourself a little grace and be gentle.

\* \* \*

As you step into your power, start showing and teaching others, if they are open to it. This will help in the flow of your own purpose and power.

Some of those questions you ask yourself will not align with others. This is a very normal process in stepping into your power. For most of your life, you have not done this. This means that those who have had control over your life, (this is including your mind, body, soul) are very fear driven. They meant well and thought it was best for you at the time. Let go of any resentment and anger towards them or yourself.

Take time to spend meditating with yourself so that your "team" can understand that they are all together in this process. This helps quiet the mind, body and soul.

Remember, your life is never ending. There is no end point. It is always evolving. You are allowed to change your situation at any time. Knowing this helps you take risks. Venture out! Know that you can always come back to your center point.

**You are now ready to be Authentically You!®**

# ABOUT THE AUTHOR

Amelia Krabach is the creator of the *Authentically You!*® program and a lifelong guide in spiritual healing, energy work, and personal transformation. With over 20 years of experience as a Reiki Master, teacher, and healer, Amelia empowers individuals to reconnect with who they truly are beneath the noise of expectation and past experiences.

Through her company, Team You LLC, she has built a community dedicated to emotional, mental, physical, and spiritual alignment. Her teachings draw from a wide range of wisdom traditions, including Qabalistic studies, and are rooted in the belief that authenticity is the key to wholeness.

*Authentically You!* is more than a book—it's a movement to help people remember their worth, trust their inner voice, and live a life that reflects their truth. Amelia lives in Novi, Michigan, with her husband Sean, their dog Finnegan, and their cat Benny, and continues to mentor a growing network of energy workers around the world. More information and classes can be found at theteamyou.com.

# ACKNOWLEDGMENTS

I would first like to thank Carly Richards for helping me come up with the name Authentically You!. She was my first student in the course and after taking it helped me realize that the other title, which I can't even remember, was too wordy.

I'd also like to thank Cari Kussy for helping get me out running, which truly helped solidify the internal ideas for this book.

I'd like to thank my husband, Sean Krabach for always supporting me and allowing me to be silly, loud, and exploratory, my core words.

I'd like to thank all of those students who took my early courses, the five, six, eight different renditions of this class, even those who've taken it more than once, I appreciate you all. Authentically You! is a life experience and these tools I use every day. My mind, Mindy, my soul, Saul, and my body, Brody, are my best friends. They never leave me. You're never alone as long as you trust, love, and honor those parts of you.

I'd also like to thank Amanda Dana for helping me with the first and second, maybe even third draft of this book, and then realizing I needed to scrap it all because it wasn't really authentic. It wasn't my silly, loud exploratory self and that this version reflects more of who I am.

# AVOIDANCE

Welcome to the last chapter of this book. If you've read all the way through, congratulations! This chapter is here as a reminder that in the future, you may deal with a little bit of this energy. So, I'm going to help you with that.

If you just flipped to the end of this book and wanted to see what this last chapter was all about, exactly what it's about, avoidance. What are you afraid of attempting? Are you fearful of getting to really know yourself? Are you afraid that once you discover your authentic self, you actually have to be that and discard the people and places and things that don't resonate with you. Authentically You! is a process. It's an entire experience of shifting, altering, and adapting to what's truly yours, your true self.

So don't forget your mind, your body, your soul, your internal compasses. Remember, the external world is not your compass. If you are avoiding something, it's because you have refused to listen to your children: your mind, your body and your soul.

It's hard to haul them around day after day when you don't listen; so listen to what they need and try the following techniques. If you don't know what these techniques are it's because you went to the end of the book and that's OK too.

This is about the exploration of yourself and the discovering that these techniques really do work if you truly listen. Discovering this chapter is letting you know that you are being guided by your higher self.

# SETTING UP GOOD PRACTICES

## Amnesia

It's perfectly fine to have amnesia with yourself every day. What I mean is that you can start fresh all over and forgive what you didn't know yesterday and try again today. Start fresh with no residual hate or anger towards self for the things you think you failed to do or experience.

## Love yourself

Be gentle with your parts. Say you're sorry and try to be more loving if you keep repeating the same mistake. The gentleness you exude towards yourself will eventually help you towards achieving the best parts of you.

## Do one thing for each part

Really try to include your mind, body and soul everyday even if it's only for 15 minutes. By separating out individual experiences or listening differently to each part of you, you will begin to understand how you operate and what are your triggers.

### 3-day rule

Having an awareness of when you are repeating patterns can keep you out of the mud. Be accountable when you are repeating habits or things 3 days in a row. Generally, this can be the first indicator you are falling back into your old ways of existence.

### Open yourself to the quiet part of you

We all have moments when the time out is needed. Look for those cues in your own life. A fifteen minute solace of quiet time a few days a week can do wonders for the parts of you that need balance.

### Live your core words

Really try to not feel like your core words need to be altered. You are you because of these descriptions. They are not bad or faulty. They are you and when you embrace them they are liberating. So liberate you!

### Embrace your non-copied self

You are you for a reason. Focus on your thinking and experiences in life by living by your authentic self, Authentically You!

www.ingramcontent.com/pod-product-compliance
Lightning Source LLC
Chambersburg PA
CBHW060632130626
46555CB00002B/768